We are met on a great battle-field of that war. We have come to dedicate a portion of that field, as a final resting place for those who here gave their lives that that nation might live. It is altogether fitting and proper that we should do this.

But, in a larger sense, we can not dedicate - we can not consecrate - we can not hallow this ground. The brave men, living and dead, who struggled here, have consecrated it, far above our poor power to add or detract.

Abraham Lincoln
Gettysburg Address
November 19, 1863

Gettysburg

Perspectives of the Battlefield, the Town, and the Sacred Landscape That Surrounds

Photography and Text by
Matthew A. Holzman

Bryan Farm – Located in Ziegler's Grove, the barn was used as a field hospital during the battle. On the front lines, men of the Union Second Corps defended this ground during Pickett's Charge on July 3.

Front cover: Monument to the 15th New York Independent Battery

Front insert: Statue of Abraham Lincoln outside Stevens Hall at Gettysburg College

Title spread: Hancock Avenue

Spreads:
The First Day – July 1, 1863 – Sunrise on Reynolds Avenue
The Second Day – July 2, 1863 – Intersection of Wheatfield Road and Emmitsburg Road
The Third Day – July 3, 1863 – Position of Battery A, 1st Rhode Island Light Artillery near The Angle
In and Around Town – Coster Avenue Mural

Back insert: Sunrise on East Cemetery Hill

Back cover: State of Pennsylvania Monument

Appreciation

I would like to sincerely thank the U.S. Department of the Interior, the National Park Service (NPS), Gettysburg National Military Park, the Civil War Trust, and the Borough of Gettysburg, Pennsylvania, for their past, present, and future management, preservation, and interpretation efforts. It is a true privilege for visitors to have the opportunity to absorb the monumental events that transpired on these historic fields and streets.

I also wish to acknowledge Hal Jespersen's public domain maps. I encourage anyone to use them for the further understanding and study of select Civil War battles and campaigns.

Recommended Websites

Gettysburg National Military Park – https://www.nps.gov/gett
Stone Sentinels (Steve A. Hawks) – www.stonesentinels.com
Gettysburg Daily – www.gettysburgdaily.com
Hal Jespersen's Civil War Maps – www.cwmaps.com
Civil War Trust – https://www.civilwar.org

George Weikert Farm - Occupied by Union forces, troops of the Second Corps rushed through the property while heading to the fighting in the Wheatfield on July 2. The house served as a field hospital.

Hummelbaugh Farm - Located behind Union lines on Cemetery Ridge, Confederate General William Barksdale was taken to this house after sustaining life threatening wounds on July 2. He died here later that night.

Snyder Farm - As a starting point for their assault on July 2, Confederates under General John Bell Hood marched over this ground before fighting at Little Round Top and Devil's Den.

Slyder Farm - Two Vermont companies of the Second United States Sharpshooters met the onset of Longstreet's Corps here and helped to check its advance upon the Round Tops. The farm's outbuildings became a Confederate field hospital.

Equestrian monument to Major General Winfield S. Hancock on East Cemetery Hill

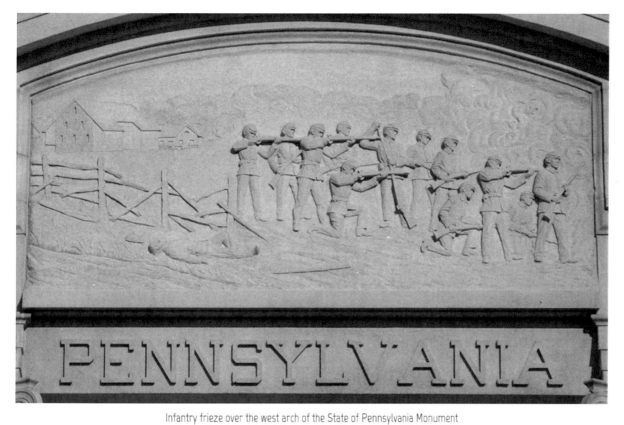

Infantry frieze over the west arch of the State of Pennsylvania Monument

Sunrise on Cemetery Ridge

Monument to Wisconsin's Company G, First United States Sharpshooters

Confederate soldier from the State of
Virginia Monument

Monument to the 78th and 102nd
New York Infantry Regiments

State of Louisiana Monument

Introduction

When the subject of Gettysburg comes up, I'm not only reminded of the first time I ever saw the movie *"Gettysburg,"* but the first few times I actually drove to see the incredible battlefield and town from Northeast Ohio. I will always vividly remember taking the Pennsylvania Turnpike to Breezewood and then meandering along U.S. Route 30 all the way past McConnellsburg, through Chambersburg, and finally on to Gettysburg. The excitement of seeing the monuments first appear on McPherson's Ridge was beyond description. In fact, it still is and will always be, wherever I may approach this amazing destination from. Additional interest in this era of history was forever heightened when I discovered that I had an ancestor who fought in this war.

My great-great-grandfather, George F. Siemon, served with the 123rd Pennsylvania Infantry. This was a nine-month unit which formed at Allegheny City in August 1862. Attached to the Third Division of the Fifth Corps in the Army of the Potomac, this regiment arrived on the field the day after Antietam, charged Marye's Heights at Fredericksburg, and was placed in a reserve position at Chancellorsville. With their term of service having expired in May 1863, these men were ordered to Harrisburg to muster out and return home. This means that my ancestor did not participate in the following campaign that culminated with this great battle in Pennsylvania. However, I can only imagine the suspense that must have gripped him and his former comrades as they read in newspapers or heard by word of mouth that their home state was being invaded. With that, it is only necessary to chart how both armies ended up at Gettysburg.

In the spring of 1863, the Confederacy had momentum and looked to build upon it. The Army of Northern Virginia, commanded by General Robert E. Lee, had defeated the Army of the Potomac at Fredericksburg in December of 1862, and at Chancellorsville in May of 1863. Once his army had gathered and been reorganized, Lee began moving his men north in early June. He hoped to draw the Federals away from Washington, D.C. and find needed supplies in the rich and untouched farmlands of Pennsylvania. It was also reasoned that one more resounding victory might pressure the United States government to seek a peace agreement with the Confederacy. Thus, the Confederates moved into Pennsylvania and eventually converged in Chambersburg. Spread out, and as Union forces approached, the road network would allow them to concentrate some 20 miles to the east, around Gettysburg. This Adams County community would never be the same.

While this specific work is not intended to be an exhaustive look at the battle and its subsequent impact on the town and surrounding area, it is meant to provide unique visual perspectives of Gettysburg's most notable monuments, farms, and other points of interest. Hopefully, some of the included imagery captured on these hallowed grounds and streets varies from that normally seen at this scenic place of American pilgrimage.

Monument to the Third Division, Fifth Corps on Crawford Avenue

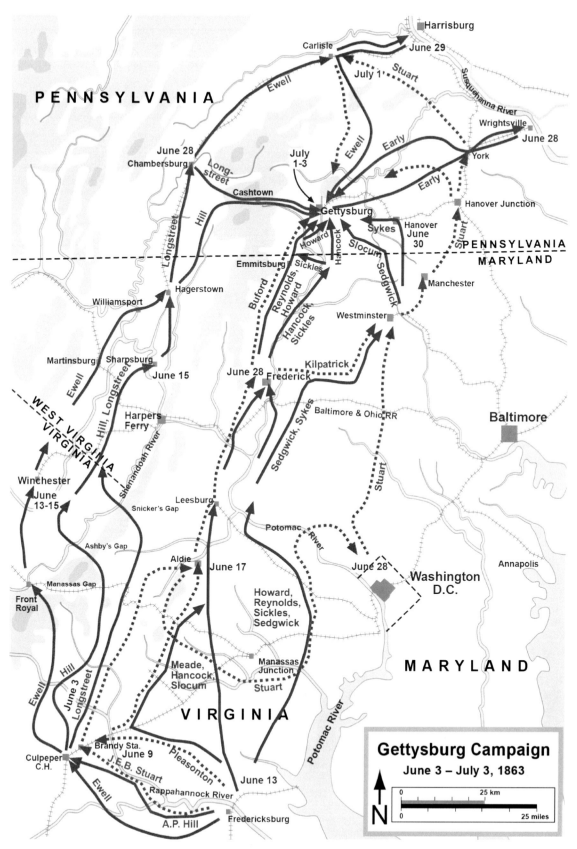

Overview of the Gettysburg Campaign (up to July 3, 1863). (Map by Hal Jespersen, www.cwmaps.com).

The town and Oak Ridge as seen from the observation tower on Culp's Hill

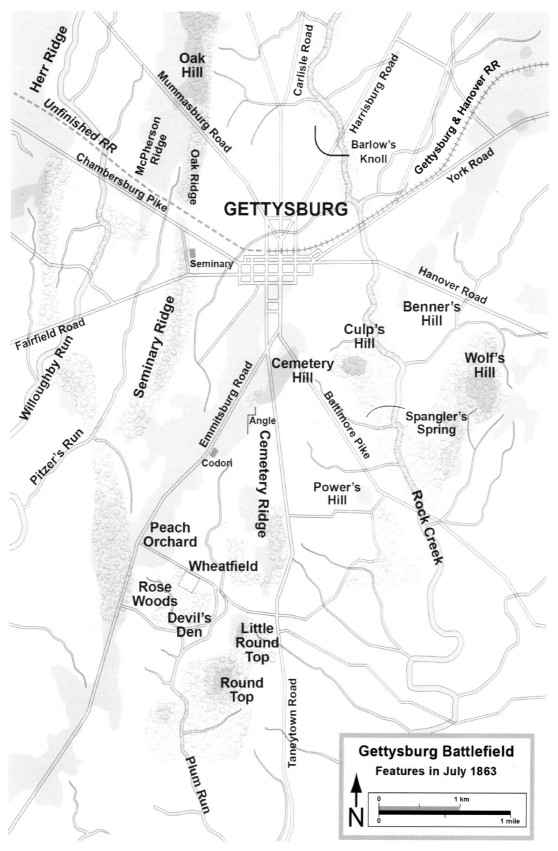

Herr Ridge

Unfinished RR

Chambersburg Pike

McPherson Ridge

Oak Ridge

Mummasburg Road

Oak Hill

Carlisle Road

Harrisburg Road

Gettysburg & Hanover RR

York Road

Barlow's Knoll

GETTYSBURG

Seminary

Fairfield Road

Willoughby Run

Pitzer's Run

Seminary Ridge

Emmitsburg Road

Angle

Codori

Cemetery Ridge

Peach Orchard

Wheatfield

Rose Woods

Devil's Den

Little Round Top

Round Top

Taneytown Road

Plum Run

Cemetery Hill

Culp's Hill

Benner's Hill

Wolf's Hill

Spangler's Spring

Baltimore Pike

Power's Hill

Rock Creek

Hanover Road

Gettysburg Battlefield

Features in July 1863

N

0   1 km

0   1 mile

Gettysburg and vicinity, July 1863. [Map by Hal Jespersen, www.cwmaps.com].

The First Day - July 1, 1863

Units of both armies first met to the west and north of town. Union cavalry slowed the Confederate advance until infantry from the First and Eleventh Corps arrived. More Southern reinforcements reached the scene, however, and by the end of the day roughly 30,000 Confederates had defeated about 20,000 Federals, driving them back through Gettysburg and on to the high ground of Cemetery Hill and Culp's Hill.

Union General John Buford and his two brigades of cavalry arrived in Gettysburg on June 30, 1863. He sent scouts out in all directions to gather intelligence on the location of enemy units. On the morning of July 1, Buford's men discovered a column of Confederates marching down the Chambersburg Turnpike.

A few miles west of town, Lieutenant Marcellus Jones of the 8th Illinois Cavalry fired what is considered to be the first shot of the battle. Years later, a small monument was placed on Knoxlyn Ridge to mark the spot. Falling back from one ridge to the next, the cavalry bought time as Union infantry rushed to the sound of the action from the south. At the base of General Buford's monument, a small bronze plaque marks the barrel that fired the first Union artillery shot. It was tracked down after the war by its serial number.

Ahead of his First Corps, General John Reynolds arrived and met Buford. Assessing the ground and situation, he decided to fight at Gettysburg as Confederates advanced in force.

Southerners of General Henry Heth's Division approached McPherson's Ridge through fields and woodlots. As fighting erupted around Edward McPherson's farm buildings, John Burns, who was a town citizen and veteran of the War of 1812, obtained a musket and insisted upon joining the Union line. He fell in with the 150th Pennsylvania and later fought with the Iron Brigade. Burns was wounded but survived to become a national celebrity. Still visible on McPherson's barn are carved initials made in 1889 by two veterans of the 143rd Pennsylvania.

McPHERSON BARN
THIS BARN WAS USED AS A HOSPITAL AND SHELTERED THE WOUNDED OF THE UNION AND CONFEDERATE ARMIES
JULY 1. 2. 3. 1863

In the Herbst Woodlot, men from Tennessee and Alabama under James Archer clashed with Federals from Michigan, Indiana, and Wisconsin in Solomon Meredith's Iron Brigade. As the fighting surged across Willoughby's Run, the 26th North Carolina sustained devastating losses. Out of 800 men taken into battle, nearly 600 were lost just on this day. Additionally, the regiment's colors were shot down over a dozen times.

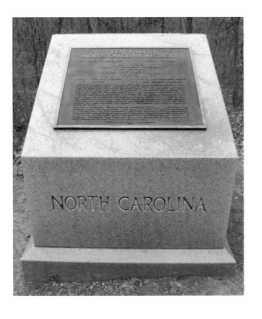

NORTH CAROLINA

As both sides rushed reinforcements into the mounting struggle, the dead and dying were strewn across McPherson's Ridge. Colonel Roy Stone's Pennsylvania Bucktails were driven back in an afternoon assault. As the Iron Brigade was initially deployed at the edge of the woods, General Reynolds rode ahead to order the "Black Hat Devils" forward.

As Reynolds turned with his back to the woods, he was struck in the head and fell from his horse. He was dead before he hit the ground. To this day, historians still disagree on the details of his death and the source of the bullet. Whatever the scenario, Reynolds was the highest ranking general officer killed at Gettysburg. For his presence on this part of the battlefield, the Pennsylvanian was honored with both an equestrian monument on the Chambersburg Pike and a smaller monument to mark the site of his death. The difficulty of command fell to Abner Doubleday.

As General Doubleday arrived on the field, Joseph Davis and his brigade of Confederates moved around and into an unfinished railroad bed that ran towards the town. To assist Lysander Cutler's Union brigade, Doubleday ordered the 6th Wisconsin of the Iron Brigade to help face the threat.

Positioned along the Chambersburg Pike, Colonel Rufus Dawes ordered his Wisconsin troops to charge the railroad cut. Joined with the 95th New York and 14th Brooklyn of Cutler's Brigade, they captured a few hundred Confederates and drove the rest out. While the cut had initially appeared to be a natural defense and beneficial for delivering fire, it proved to be a compromising position for its sides were too deep to scale in some places. It quite literally became a pit for the Mississippians who had advanced into it.

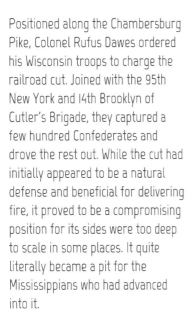

After noon, Confederate General Richard Ewell's Corps began arriving down roads from the north. On Oak Hill, Robert Rodes moved his brigades into position. Uncoordinated attacks soon followed.

When it was apparent that Southern forces had taken possession of Oak Hill, General Doubleday shifted reinforcements to meet the threat. Henry Baxter's Brigade hid behind a stone wall on the crest of Oak Ridge. Separated and exposed, General Alfred Iverson's North Carolinians took decimating fire and dropped to the ground. Hundreds were later captured. Notable monuments seen on the ridge today include that to the 11th Pennsylvania, with that regiment's fighting companion "Sallie," and the "Granite Tree" to the 90th Pennsylvania.

While Union defenders here were relieved, many had exhausted their ammunition. Additionally, they were confronted by the onslaught of Ramseur's Brigade, Iverson's remnants, and Alabamians under Colonel Edward A. O'Neal. This drove the Federals from the ridge that offers great perspectives of both the McLean Farm below and the town in the distance. Crowning Oak Hill is the Eternal Light Peace Memorial. It was dedicated in 1938 during the battle's 75th anniversary.

When Union General Oliver O. Howard's Eleventh Corps arrived, he ordered two divisions north of Gettysburg to extend the line of the First Corps. Since Confederates had already occupied Oak Hill, the Federals were vulnerable on this lower ground. General Francis Barlow's First Division advanced to a rise known as Blocher's Knoll.

Shortly thereafter, Southerners of General Jubal Early's Division arrived on the Harrisburg Road and were poised to completely overwhelm and dislodge Barlow's men. The flanking attack that ensued was spearheaded by a brigade of Georgians under John Gordon. After a short contest which left Barlow severely wounded, the entire Eleventh Corps was forced to retreat back through the streets of town. Fortunately for the Union troops in disarray, General Winfield S. Hancock was on hand to provide leadership and rallying inspiration on Cemetery Hill. As both armies concentrated, it now seemed certain that a major battle would take place at Gettysburg.

The Second Day - July 2, 1863

On the second day of battle, Union reinforcements arrived and a fish hook shaped line was formed on ground running south from Gettysburg. The Army of Northern Virginia wrapped around the Union position. This resulted with a Confederate line that was much thinner and longer. On the afternoon of July 2, Lee ordered a heavy assault on the Union's left flank, and fierce fighting raged at Devil's Den, Little Round Top, the Peach Orchard, the Wheatfield, and along Cemetery Ridge. On the Union right, demonstrations escalated into full-scale attacks on Culp's Hill and East Cemetery Hill. Although the Southerners gained ground, the Federal defenders still held strong positions at the end of the day.

Throughout the evening of July 1 and morning of July 2, most of the remaining infantry of both armies arrived on the field. The Union line ran from Culp's Hill southeast of the town to Cemetery Hill just south of town, then south for nearly two miles along Cemetery Ridge, terminating just north of Little Round Top.

The Confederate line paralleled the Union line about a mile to the west on Seminary Ridge, ran east through the town, then curved southeast to a point opposite Culp's Hill. This resulted with the Army of the Potomac having interior lines of communication while the Army of Northern Virginia was spread nearly five miles from point to point. For July 2, Lee planned a general assault on Union lines. After a long march to get in position on the enemy's left, General James Longstreet's First Corps began its attack at roughly 4:00 p.m.

Along the Emmitsburg Road was Joseph Sherfy's peach orchard. To Union General Dan Sickles, the orchard's elevation could provide his Third Corps with a better overall position to meet a flanking attack.

Without orders from General George Meade, who was now in command of the entire Army of the Potomac, Sickles broke formation and moved his line forward, forming a sharp right angle at the orchard. This meant that his men were susceptible to attack from two sides. After initial Confederate artillery fire, General William Barksdale's Mississippians smashed into the Federals and sent them back. At the Trostle Farm in the rear, Sickles was struck in the leg by a solid artillery shot and carried from the field. The barn still displays prime evidence from the battle.

To the south, General Joseph Kershaw's South Carolina brigade swept over the fields of the Rose Farm. Under heavy artillery to the front, they were eventually joined by troops from Georgia under General Paul Semmes. With the Southerners capturing Sherfy's peach orchard and threatening elsewhere in force, word quickly reached the main Union line on Cemetery Ridge that Sickles had created a gap in need of support. Following the battle, photographer Alexander Gardner captured several scenes of the dead on the Rose Farm.

The action moved through woodlots and into "The Wheatfield." Owned by the Rose family, this 20 acre field changed hands at least six times. There were several attacks and counterattacks by mixed units. The third phase of this confusing "whirlpool" saw General John Caldwell's Second Corps division push Confederates back toward the Rose Farm. Additional reinforcements from the Fifth Corps arrived but they were eventually overrun. In all, over 6,000 men became casualties in this area. A very distinguishable monument here honors the Irish Brigade. It features a Celtic Cross and wolfhound.

Another ramification of the Union Third Corps collapse along the Emmitsburg Road was that the main Union line on Cemetery Ridge became heavily threatened. Most of the Federals from the Second Corps had been sent to "The Wheatfield" and other areas, leaving the center to be very diminished. As Confederate General Cadmus Wilcox's Alabama brigade was rushing to exploit the gap, General Winfield S. Hancock approached the 1st Minnesota and realized these were the only troops immediately available. He ordered the regiment to charge and stall the rapidly advancing enemy. Of the 262 men who did charge, only 47 returned. The 1st Minnesota's sacrifice bought critical time for the Union.

Shortly after Confederate General John Bell Hood arrived on Warfield Ridge with his division, he became skeptical of the exposed and rough ground his men would have to traverse. He shared his frustrations for the orders with General Longstreet. Since the overall assault was already delayed with Lee's intentions, Longstreet overruled.

Included in Hood's Division was General Evander Law's Alabama brigade. The State of Alabama erected a monument to commemorate these troops and mark the location where they began their attack. Moving across the Bushman Farm, Hood's men were soon under musket and artillery fire from beyond. When Sickles had advanced his Third Corps forward from Cemetery Ridge, his brigade under General John H. H. Ward occupied a grouping of large rocks forever known as "Devil's Den." The guns of Captain James E. Smith's New York battery were brought up.

During their advance, the Southerners became intermingled but were able to capture the crest of Devil's Den. In the process, Smith's Battery lost three of its four guns.

Georgians of Henry L. Benning's Brigade arrived and overwhelmed the area. Confederate sharpshooters would go on to use the cover that Devil's Den provided for targeting Union troops on Little Round Top. As they proceeded through the valley below, the men of the 48th and 44th Alabama covered even more rugged terrain. For this, and the dead left behind, this gorge was described as a "Slaughter Pen." In the woods above, Texans skirmished at another set of irregular rocks known as the "Devil's Kitchen" and Law's Alabamians scaled Big Round Top.

All of the initial Union movements had left the dominant heights of Little Round Top abandoned. Gouverneur K. Warren, Chief Engineer of the Army of the Potomac, was sent by General Meade to assess the situation. Shocked to find no infantry on this elevated position, Warren and his staff desperately searched for reinforcements. The Fifth Corps brigades under Colonel Strong Vincent and General Stephen Weed arrived on the hill just before the Confederates emerged.

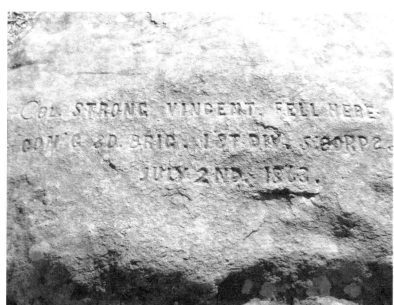

Union sharpshooters and the challenging ground slowed the Alabama and Texas troops who had already marched roughly twenty miles on this hot day. Men from New York, Pennsylvania, Maine, and Michigan held against and regrouped for several Confederate thrusts. With a desperate bayonet charge, the 20th Maine finally drove off the 15th Alabama. Another daring counterattack was made by the 140th New York. Exhausted, the Confederates reluctantly withdrew. The Union brought up additional support and now occupied Little Round Top in force.

During the fight, Colonel Vincent was mortally wounded as he attempted to rally the men of his brigade. Removed from the field, he was recommended for promotion to Brigadier General and died on July 7. His unofficial likeness is represented on the monument to the 83rd Pennsylvania. Even though Little Round Top appears to be a prime artillery position, its rocky and narrow crest limited the number of guns that were able to be manhandled up and put into line to effectively fire. The hill's steep slopes prevented Union gunners from depressing their barrels enough. However, the guns here would be able to deliver more distant fire on the battle's last day.

When Longstreet's assault opened on the Federal left, General Richard S. Ewell ordered Major Joseph Latimer's artillery battalion to fire upon gun positions on the Union right. On the evening of July I, General Edward Johnson's Confederate division had marched through town and occupied a position along the Hanover Road.

While Latimer's fire was meant to serve as a diversion, several Union pieces positioned on Cemetery Hill and Culp's Hill soon responded. An artillery duel ensued. As the attention of the Federals had been gained, casualties began to mount for the Southerners. Major Latimer, only 19 years of age, was mortally wounded. After the firing ceased, three brigades under Johnson moved out in preparation to attack the entrenched Union position on the wooded slopes of Culp's Hill. To do so, they would have to cross Rock Creek. The stream ran at the base of the hill and proved formidable.

In the morning, the Union Twelfth Corps under General Henry Slocum had been ordered to take position on Culp's Hill and extend the line to the Baltimore Pike near Rock Creek.

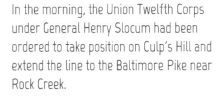

To counter what was assumed to be Longstreet's more threatening assault, General Meade stripped Slocum's Corps of troops and began transferring them to the left. This left General George Greene's brigade of New Yorkers behind to further construct and strengthen fortifications. For this work, rocks and trees were plentiful here. Greene had to defend the entire line from the summit of Culp's Hill to Spangler's Spring, an area that was popular for local picnicking. Numerically inferior, but assisted by the breastworks, Greene's men would fight into the night.

Once again, Cemetery Hill became the focus. Two brigades of Confederate infantry under Colonel Isaac Avery and General Harry T. Hays moved outside of town and advanced over rolling fields against Union gun emplacements. On a nearby knoll described early as "McKnight's Hill," the 5th Maine Battery had helped to silence Latimer's guns. Now, as Avery's North Carolinians marched, the battery delivered enfilade fire down their ranks. The knoll was later renamed "Stevens' Knoll" for the battery's commander.

Positioned around the gatehouse to the Evergreen Cemetery, the already depleted men of the Union Eleventh Corps were surprised by the valiant determination of the Confederates. Working their way up the slopes, elements of Avery's North Carolina Tarheels and Hays' Louisiana Tigers broke through and captured a number of Union guns on the crest of the hill. A bitter struggle was remembered by many. Eventually, the Federals were aided by timely reinforcements and the Confederates were forced to retire. The line was secured.

During the night of July 2, General Meade summoned the army's respective corps commanders to his headquarters along the Taneytown Road. Inside Lydia Leister's small farmhouse, the Union generals decided to vote on their next moves. After much conversation and assessment, it was decided by most to "stay and fight it out." Meade now had a better understanding of both the gains his army made and losses they sustained. The overall position could not be vacated given the day's events. Similarly on the Confederate side, General Lee measured what had occurred after hitting the enemy's flanks. A course of action for the following day awaited.

The Third Day - July 3, 1863

On July 3, morning fighting resumed on Culp's Hill, and cavalry engaged to the east and south, but the main action was a forward infantry assault made by more than 12,000 Confederates against the Union center on Cemetery Ridge. "Pickett's Charge," as it is now known, was repulsed by Union forces. The Army of Northern Virginia suffered unimaginable losses.

Throughout the early hours of July 3, many of the troops that had been sent south from the Culp's Hill area to support the Union left began to return. General Lee's initial plan was to renew his attacks by coordinating the action on Culp's Hill with another attack by Generals Longstreet and A.P. Hill against Cemetery Ridge.

At dawn, Union batteries opened fire on Confederates who had captured positions on lower Culp's Hill and around Spangler's Spring the day before. With this, effective fire came from Powers' Hill. There, the Federals had two full batteries consisting of a dozen field pieces. The Union attack did not accommodate Lee. General Ewell even felt that it was too late to recall his men. A specifically futile assault was made by two Union regiments near Spangler's Spring. The 2nd Massachusetts and 27th Indiana were heavily repulsed by those Confederates behind the works.

Across a traverse dividing upper and lower Culp's Hill is the monument to the Confederate 2nd Maryland Infantry (1st Maryland Battalion). It became the first Confederate monument on the field.

Despite attempting multiple assaults, Johnson's men were beaten back with terrible losses all along the line. Greene's breastworks had proved to be invaluable. The struggle for Culp's Hill finally phased out around noon and was the longest sustained fight during the battle. Meanwhile, a few miles east of town along the Hanover Road, Confederate General J.E.B. Stuart had finally arrived with his cavalry units and looked to harass the Union rear. In notable action, David McM. Gregg ordered George Custer's Michigan troopers to counterattack around John Rummel's Farm.

After Union horsemen had checked Stuart's initial advances, Wade Hampton's men were then sent in to only be caught up in a violent collision and surrounded. The Southern cavaliers were forced to withdraw. Strategically, Lee's plans now shifted. After defeating Union forces on July I, and hitting the flanks throughout, he reasoned that a blow to the center on Cemetery Ridge might create the breach his army could exploit. Around I p.m., over I50 Confederate guns began an artillery bombardment.

In order to save valuable ammunition for the infantry attack that they suspected would follow, the Federal artillery, under the command of General Henry Hunt, initially held its fire. Eventually, dozens of pieces responded. Many of the Confederate rounds overshot their targets and landed around General Meade's headquarters along the Taneytown Road. In the woods on Seminary Ridge, over 12,000 men from North Carolina, Tennessee, Florida, Virginia, Alabama, and Mississippi were preparing to step out and advance to Cemetery Ridge.

Organizationally, General Longstreet was placed at the head of three divisions that would be led by Generals George Pickett, J. Johnston Pettigrew, and Isaac Trimble. These commands consisted of troops from Longstreet's own First Corps and A.P. Hill's Third Corps. History seems to reflect that Longstreet could not see the success of such an endeavor and certainly shied away from its theory. Pickett's Virginians had arrived on the field the day before and were the freshest troops available for the attack. When Pickett approached Longstreet for permission to lead his men forward, Longstreet only nodded. Around 3 p.m., the cannon fire subsided. It was time to move out.

The distance in which the Confederates had to march combined with the open ground that was scaled in by many waiting Union Second Corps soldiers added up to a hopeless action. Dedicated in 1917, the State of Virginia Monument on Seminary Ridge was the first of the Confederate State monuments to be placed at Gettysburg.

After many Union gunners had opened with counter fire of their own during the cannonade, many were ordered to fall silent. This was an act of deception to make the Confederates believe that the guns along certain points of the line had been knocked out. It worked. Out across the fields the Southerners marched. Their muskets gleamed and their flags waved. Soon enough, shells began to tear holes in the ranks. As the men fell, the lines were filled. Advancing under constant fire, they were severely slowed by fences.

The historic Emmitsburg Road bisects these fields. When Pickett's men reached the road, they performed a left oblique and passed by the Codori Farm. Even more rail fences had to be toppled.

In front of the main Union defense, the 8th Ohio Infantry had been placed out in the fields beyond the Emmitsburg Road. As Pettigrew's force surged toward them, the 8th fired into the flank of John Brockenbrough's surprised Virginians, who broke back to Seminary Ridge. The 8th then turned and continued to fire into advancing North Carolinians and Mississippians. Despite only having 160 men, these Buckeyes took over 300 prisoners and captured the colors of a few Confederate regiments.

Battery A, 4th United States Artillery, commanded by Lt. Alonzo H. Cushing, was positioned behind a bend in a stone wall known as "The Angle." Confederate artillery fire had done considerable damage to Cushing's Battery, killing many of his horses and exploding his ammunition. Miraculously, about two hundred men actually made it all the way up to the wall. As they did, an already grievously wounded Cushing fired his last round of canister and was struck one last time, falling dead beside his guns.

In some cases, the fighting was hand-to-hand. The farthest advance into Union lines was led by General Lewis Armistead of Pickett's Division. After a terrific struggle, Armistead fell mortally wounded and consuming Union forces rallied. Those Confederates who were not killed were captured. By 4 p.m., the surviving men who had risked everything for home and country were in a disorganized retreat back to Seminary Ridge. The devastation was staggering. Out of the more than 12,000 who started across these fields, over half became casualties. General Lee rode out to meet some of those who did return.

This momentous attack is forever enshrined as "Pickett's Charge." While Pickett never forgave Lee for the loss his division suffered that day, Lee never forgave himself. The defeat was crippling on the Confederacy. For the remainder of the war, the Army of Northern Virginia was theoretically on the defensive. After more than 50,000 casualties on both sides, the Union had remained intact and the Army of the Potomac had finally won a major victory. Dedicated in 1910 on Cemetery Ridge, the State of Pennsylvania Monument is the largest on the battlefield. Nearly one out of every three Union soldiers here came from Pennsylvania. Over 34,000 of their names are listed around the monument.

154TH NEW YORK
INFANTRY.
1ST BRIGADE, 2ND DIVISION
11TH CORPS.
JULY 1, 1863.

In and Around Town

Due to the modern commercialism that is an inescapable reality of Gettysburg today, many visitors view the town only through that lens. While many historically themed shops and restaurants make up a significant part of this community's identity, it should be remembered that shot and shell also disrupted the lives of those who lived here in July 1863. The town may not be recognized as being on the heart of the battlefield but it was very much a part of the battle. One can only imagine the terrifying prospect of a family being forced to leave their home as two great armies surrounded it in the midst of a great war. Many of the area's structures still allow us to get a glimpse at what those citizens had to endure.

Located about eight miles west of Gettysburg is the historic Cashtown Inn. This building operated as a tavern for decades before the battle. Sitting along the mountain road between Chambersburg and Gettysburg, thousands of Confederates passed by the structure during the campaign.

On the morning of July 1, General Lee conferred with General A.P. Hill in front of the Inn as the sounds of battle could be heard a few miles east. Today, the Cashtown Inn is a very popular bed and breakfast destination. On the outskirts of town on the Chambersburg Turnpike was the Sheads House. The Oak Ridge Seminary, a finishing school for young ladies, was opened in this building by Carrie Sheads in 1862. The house became a hospital as over 70 wounded soldiers were treated here. An embedded artillery shell can still be seen to the left of the top window.

Mary Thompson's home was selected by General Lee's staff for headquarters. It was situated at the center of the Confederate line that took shape during the battle and was on high ground.

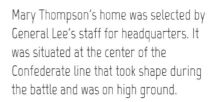

Arriving on the afternoon of July I, Lee saw the Federals get driven through town. While he did go inside Thompson's home, it is believed that he slept in his tent. His headquarters marker is located right across the Chambersburg Pike. Nearby on Seminary Ridge was Schmucker Hall or the "Old Dorm." This was the center of the Lutheran Theological Seminary. The building's cupola was used as an observation post by Union General John Buford.

North of town off the old Harrisburg Road are both Jones Avenue and the Josiah Benner Farm. Rarely seen by visitors, the farm was a field hospital and the avenue marks where Confederate artillery under Hilary Jones exchanged fire with Union guns on Barlow's Knoll. Near a brickyard on the northern edge of town, the 154th New York made a stand on July 1. A mural at the end of Coster Avenue depicts that struggle. A mile to the east, Johnson's Confederates moved past the Daniel Lady Farm before attacking Culp's Hill.

Some of the town's most visible battle damage survives on the walls of both the Stock House and the Farnsworth House. Located on South Washington Street, Jacob Stock's home was at the center of skirmishing between William D. Pender's Confederates and Adolph von Steinwehr's Federals. Named for General Elon J. Farnsworth, who was killed in a cavalry charge on July 3, the Farnsworth House sits along Baltimore Street. With a clear view of Cemetery Hill during the battle, Confederate sharpshooters used it for shelter. Today, the house is a popular dining attraction and serves as a bed and breakfast.

Since the Army of the Potomac held the field after the battle, its men were left with the treatment of the remaining wounded. On July 5, 1863, orders were issued to establish a hospital somewhere around Gettysburg. On the York Pike about a mile and a half east of town, a site was chosen. The hospital was named after the Medical Director of the Army of the Potomac, Dr. Jonathan Letterman. Spread across fields of the George Wolf Farm, it was near the main road so that supplies could be brought in to those in need. Additionally, a railroad depot was established to further assist the site with overall transportation. Today, a marker stands where the vast "Camp Letterman" was located.

On the evening of November 18, 1863, President Abraham Lincoln arrived at Gettysburg's railroad station aboard a decorated train from Washington, D.C. He traveled here to help dedicate the new National Cemetery. For months following the battle, thousands of wounded soldiers boarded trains and departed here.

On July 1, the town's center square was a scene of sure confusion as troops of the Union's First and Eleventh Corps were retreating south toward Cemetery Hill. Many smaller fights erupted in streets and alleys. Countless homes became compromised and many families were displaced. As Confederate forces pursued the Federals, artillery shots were fired across the square and several more structures were hit. For tourist attractions, some shells were later placed in the sides of buildings by the town's citizens.

The most well-known building in Gettysburg is the Wills House. As the home of attorney David Wills and his family, President Lincoln stayed here overnight as an honored guest.

Wills was very instrumental in helping to establish the Soldiers' National Cemetery. Like many other Pennsylvanians, he thought it was only necessary to provide a burial ground for the Union men who perished. During his stay in the house, it is believed that Lincoln touched up and rehearsed the text of his speech. The following morning, on November 19, 1863, Lincoln and his accompanying party would mount horses and proceed through town to the cemetery. Today, the house serves as a museum. Outside, a statue of Lincoln greets a modern visitor.

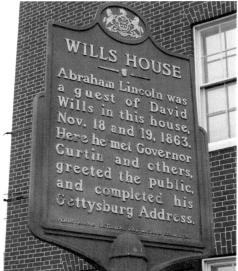

WILLS HOUSE

Abraham Lincoln was a guest of David Wills in this house, Nov. 18 and 19, 1863. Here he met Governor Curtin and others, greeted the public, and completed his Gettysburg Address.

ABRAHAM LINCOLN SLEPT IN THIS HOUSE NOVEMBER 18. 1863. THE NIGHT BEFORE HIS IMMORTAL ADDRESS AT THE CEMETERY

Perhaps the most visited attraction in town is the house on Baltimore Street where civilian Jennie Wade was killed. On the morning of July 3, she was hit by Confederate fire in the home's kitchen while baking bread for nearby Union soldiers. Her grave is in Evergreen Cemetery. Not far from where Jennie fell is a living witness to the dramatic events of 1863. Located directly across from the Farnsworth House, a large sycamore tree survives. It was standing during the battle and would have been passed by Abraham Lincoln.

WITNESS TREE

THIS SYCAMORE IS A LIVING WITNESS TO THE BATTLE OF GETTYSBURG. ABRAHAM LINCOLN PASSED BY THIS TREE ON HIS WAY TO GIVE THE GETTYSBURG ADDRESS ON NOVEMBER 19, 1863.

From the southwest end of the battlefield, you can take Millerstown Road to see Sachs Covered Bridge. In doing so, you will pass General and President Dwight D. Eisenhower's farm. Eisenhower used the farm as his presidential and retirement home. After purchasing the nearly 200-acre farm in 1950, he often relaxed here with his wife and First Lady Mamie, and their family. The Eisenhowers hosted many world leaders. Dwight, fascinated by history himself, enjoyed showing his guests around the battlefield. On July 2, 1863, Confederate troops would have marched right through his property.

Following the battle, Sachs Covered Bridge carried a large portion of Lee's retreating army over Marsh Creek. Two brigades of the Union's First Corps also crossed the bridge on July 1 as they headed towards Gettysburg. The structure was built in 1852 and has been designated as Pennsylvania's most historic bridge. It suffered flood damage in 1996 but has since been restored. While the bridge is not located on the immediate battlefield, it receives many visitors to this day.

Gettysburg National Cemetery contains more than 6,000 graves. From the Civil War, over 3,500 Union soldiers rest here. Nearly half remain unknown. Shortly after the battle, Andrew Curtin, the Governor of Pennsylvania, visited Gettysburg and saw that bodies of soldiers had been quickly put in the ground.

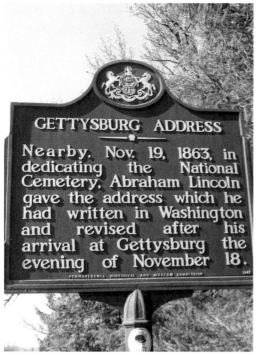

With the help of representatives from other Northern states, Curtin took the initiative to establish a new Soldiers' National Cemetery. Beginning in October 1863, remains were carefully removed from the battlefield and re-interred here. This task alone took several months. On November 19, 1863, the town's citizens, veterans from the battle, and officials from government gathered to dedicate the cemetery. It is thought that some 20,000 individuals were in attendance.

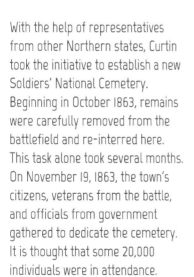

Forever known as his "Gettysburg Address," Lincoln eloquently voiced the reasons for assembling here and completely channeled the enduring necessity for a unified nation.

Edward Everett, a noted orator of the day, spoke for two hours before Lincoln. Expressing his admiration for Lincoln's words, Everett later said, "I should be glad, if I could flatter myself that I came as near to the central idea of the occasion, in two hours, as you did in two minutes." Within the cemetery today, a monument commemorates Lincoln's Address. The speech itself was delivered a few hundred yards away. The Soldiers' National Monument marks the general spot where the speaker's stand was located.

Army of Northern Virginia

General Robert E. Lee, Commanding
Strength: 72,000 men, 280 guns
Casualties: 3,903 killed, 18,735 wounded, 5,425 captured or missing, 28,063 total

FIRST CORPS
LT. GEN. JAMES LONGSTREET

McLaws' Division
Kershaw, Barksdale, Wofford, Semmes
Pickett's Division
Garnett, Kemper, Armistead
Hood's Division
Law, Robertson, Anderson, Benning
Artillery Reserve (Walton)
Alexander, Eshleman

SECOND CORPS
LT. GEN. RICHARD S. EWELL

Early's Division
Gordon, Hoke, Smith, Hays
Johnson's Division
Steuart, Walker, Nicholls, Jones
Rodes' Division
Daniel, O'Neal, Doles, Iverson, Ramseur
Artillery Reserve (Brown)
Dance, Nelson

THIRD CORPS
LT. GEN. AMBROSE P. HILL

Anderson's Division
Wilcox, Posey, Mahone, Wright, Perry
Heth's Division
Pettigrew, Brockenbrough, Archer, Davis
Pender's Division
Perrin, Lane, Thomas, Scales
Artillery Reserve (Walker)
McIntosh, Pegram

CAVALRY CORPS
MAJ. GEN. JAMES E. B. STUART

Hampton, Robertson, Fitz Lee, Jenkins,
Jones, Chambliss, Imboden,
Horse Artillery (Beckham)

Friend to Friend Masonic Memorial in the National Cemetery Annex

Army of the Potomac

Major General George G. Meade, Commanding
Strength: 93,000 men, 372 guns
Casualties: 3,155 killed, 14,529 wounded, 5,365 captured or missing, 23,049 total

FIRST CORPS
MAJ. GEN. JOHN F. REYNOLDS

First Division (Wadsworth)
Meredith, Cutler
Second Division (Robinson)
Paul, Baxter
Third Division (Doubleday)
Biddle, Stone, Stannard
Artillery Reserve (Wainwright)

SECOND CORPS
MAJ. GEN. WINFIELD S. HANCOCK

First Division (Caldwell)
Cross, Kelly, Zook, Brooke
Second Division (Gibbon)
Harrow, Webb, Hall
Third Division (Hays)
Carroll, Smyth, Willard
Artillery Reserve (Hazard)

THIRD CORPS
MAJ. GEN. DANIEL E. SICKLES

First Division (Birney)
Graham, Ward, de Trobriand
Second Division (Humphreys)
Carr, Brewster, Burling
Artillery Reserve (Randolph)

FIFTH CORPS
MAJ. GEN. GEORGE SYKES

First Division (Barnes)
Tilton, Sweitzer, Vincent
Second Division (Ayres)
Day, Burbank, Weed
Third Division (Crawford)
McCandless, Fisher
Artillery Reserve (Martin)

SIXTH CORPS
MAJ. GEN. JOHN SEDGWICK

First Division (Wright)
Torbert, Bartlett, Russell
Second Division (Howe)
Grant, Neill
Third Division (Newton)
Shaler, Eustis, Wheaton
Artillery Reserve (Tompkins)

ELEVENTH CORPS
MAJ. GEN. OLIVER O. HOWARD

First Division (Barlow)
von Gilsa, Ames
Second Division (von Steinwehr)
Coster, Smith
Third Division (Schurz)
Schimmelfennig, Krzyzanowski
Artillery Reserve (Osborn)

TWELFTH CORPS
MAJ. GEN. HENRY W. SLOCUM

First Division (Williams)
McDougall, Lockwood, Ruger
Second Division (Geary)
Candy, Cobham, Greene
Artillery Reserve (Muhlenberg)

CAVALRY CORPS
MAJ. GEN. ALFRED PLEASONTON

First Division (Buford)
Gamble, Devin, Merritt
Second Division (Gregg)
McIntosh, Huey, Gregg
Third Division (Kilpatrick)
Farnsworth, Custer
Horse Artillery
Robertson, Tidball

ARTILLERY RESERVE
BRIG. GEN. ROBERT O. TYLER

Ransom, McGilvery, Taft,
Huntington, Fitzhugh

Monument to Brigadier General Samuel Crawford

Originally from North Royalton, Ohio, Matthew A. Holzman received a Bachelor of Arts degree in History from Shepherd University in West Virginia. Stemming from his education and interests, he worked as an interpretive Park Ranger at Arlington House, The Robert E. Lee Memorial, and published the books "Civil Warscapes: Images of American Sanctuaries, Eastern Theater 1861-1863," "Civil Warscapes: Antietam, Images from the 17th of September," and "Shenandoah: A Seasonal Beckoning." While visiting several historic sites and battlefields, he goes out of his way to trace his great-great-grandfather's very steps at places like Antietam, Fredericksburg, and Chancellorsville. During the war, this same ancestor allegedly met and talked to Abraham Lincoln. Born three weeks early, Matthew believes that it might have been only fate that he was born on July 3, the same date as the last day of the Battle of Gettysburg and "Pickett's Charge." He currently resides in Manassas, Virginia.

*The world will little note, nor long remember
what we say here, but it can never forget
what they did here.*

Abraham Lincoln
Gettysburg Address
November 19, 1863

CPSIA information can be obtained
at www.ICGtesting.com
Printed in the USA
BVRC092026130122
626154BV00005B/187